Little does Zam know, her dad isn't just out to get her. He may be a little pushy, but his demands do hold some wisdom in the end. No amount of grounding and yelling will change a teenage zombie girl's mind, though; she has to do that for herself. Will Zam decide to trust and appreciate her dad before she gets into trouble she can't get out of? And will she ever convince her dad to give her a little more freedom? Amusing antics, distressing scenarios, and father-daughter frustrations are abound in Zam's world as both struggle to give the other some food for thought.

Day 1

Grounded again.

Last night at dinner I told dad I didn't want brains.

"Real zombies eat BRAINS and only BRAINS and that's that!"

It's just the same thing every time. He never explains why I'm not allowed to have other stuff and just grounds me. He put me in my room with a villager and told me I was grounded until I ate his brains and turned him into a zombie.

He even put the iron door on! Talk about ridiculous.

Diary of A Minecraft Zombie Girl

(Unofficial Minecraft Book)

Copyright © 2015 by Ian The Minecrafter

DIARY OF A MINECRAFT ZOMBIE GIRL

Zam has a problem. Lots of problems, actually –

life as a teenage zombie chick isn't easy after all.

She's always getting in trouble with her dad for

eating things like apples, steak, sugar, and

basically everything besides brains. Zam thinks

he's stuck in the past, and ends up spending a

lot of time grounded. Between punishments and

the start of school, though, she finds time to

sneak off, try new foods, hang out with her

friends, and learn that her stubborn father is just

one of her many worries as a youth growing up

in a blocky world.

I mean, I'm not one of those anti-brains activists or anything. I'm not out picketing in the sun and getting arrested by skeleton jockeys. He should be thankful. It's just that ever since Old Witch Hagatha came over to babysit and let me try some fish and flowers I've wanted to try new food.

I can't tell dad that, though. He'd fire her in an instant and she's really nice.

Day 2

Yes! Frosty came through for me once again.
Best snow golem in the world!

Frosty and I have been friends since he was a
pumpkin and I was a baby. I was afraid to tell
him why I kept getting grounded because I
didn't want him to think I was weird... But he
totally understood! Not only that, but today he
busted me outta zombie jail!

Dad woke me up this evening and handed me a shovel. He had to go to work, and he said he'd let me off early if I got rid of the snow on our sidewalk. Took me like 10 seconds! Good ol' Frosty was waiting for me at the end of the sidewalk. He said he'll come back tomorrow and throw more snow around if I come hang out with him.

I'm gonna see if dad will let me spend the day at his house tomorrow.

Day 3

Okay, you know how I said Frosty was the best snow golem? Well he's not. I mean, he's a pretty *cool* guy (ha-ha, get it?), but his dad is AWESOME!

I got to hang out with Frosty all day and he told his dad why I was grounded. I got kinda scared because, well, he's actually pretty scary if you don't know him. But he said he knew just the thing for me, and made us some snow slushies. Even if he put some brains in mine it was still super good!

It started raining, we had to go inside so Frosty

didn't melt and didn't get much time to play

outside. But the slushie seriously made my day.

Best. Dad. Ever.

Why can't my dad be more like him? Less

grounding, more slushies!

Oh, also, Frosty gave me a sweet pumpkin

helmet to wear. Now we're twins!

Day 4

Uuuggghhhh. Or at least that's what dad says

I'm supposed to say when I'm frustrated.

Dad ate the villager that he stuck in my room

and turned him into a zombie, so now we have a

stupid big-nosed creep moping around. I mean,

not a creep – I would never disrespect my

creeper buddies. Just… He's annoying.

I'm going to see if Old Man Slimus has any spare

leads, or at least if he could make me one. I

know it's cruel to just throw him out right after

he turned but I can't take another second of this

guy. I have a pretty good plan.

I'll see Old Witch Hagatha and get a splash potion of weakness from her. Then I'll tie him up outside Steve's (at the stable so the sun doesn't get him) and leave the potion there, so all he has to do is get an apple to give him.

Day 5

Well, that went poorly.

Slimus and Hagatha were actually hanging out, he was helping her make some magma cream for her potions. I should've waited til he left and asked them separately, because when I asked them both at the same time they figured it out real quick.

"Now little Zambantha, you listen to your parents and be nice to him!"

Some help that witch was. Slimus said it was dangerous anyway but whatever. So is eating flowers apparently.

I'll just have to sit around and have some fascinating conversations with him to pass the time. Why, here's a great one we had just this morning!

"Uggghhh. Uuuuuugh.

"Morning. Where's my dad?"

"Uuuugggggggggggghhhhhhh."

"Okay…. What about my mom?"

"Uuuhhh…."

Yep! About as fun as talking to a cobblestone fence.

Whatever. I'm just glad dad's not making me share a room with him.

Day 6

The Endermailman dropped off a package
today. I guess mom ordered me a new leather
armor outfit to cheer me up. It's black and red,
my favorite colors. That was pretty nice of her –
she's a great mom really, it's just dad that I can't
stand sometimes. In typical dad fashion all he
did was Ugh at me when I tried it on.

Ugh to you too, dad.

I'm going over to Zombrina's later to show her
how good I look in it.

You know, now that I think about it, Zombrina and I don't really hang out much. Ever since her parents started buying her enchanted clothes she got kinda stuck up. Which is lame because she was my best friend for so long.

I mean, I have Frosty, but he's kind of a dork. Plus he's a boy, and not a zombie, so it's just not the same. You know?

Day 7

OMG!!!!

The craziest thing happened yesterday! While I
was at Zombrina's I noticed a bunch of flowers
in her room, and when I asked her why she had
so many flowers… She made me promise not to
tell – she eats them!

It was so crazy to find out that one of my friends tried different stuff too. I told her about all the stuff with my dad and we munched on a few roses. We had to hurry up and throw them in a chest though because her mom came upstairs to see if we wanted to go watch fireworks by the diamond mine. We kinda just wanted to sit around and talk so we said no thanks.

Anyway, we're gonna go see the Old Witch together next weekend. She's out of town on a business meeting with some big potions warehouse.

Day 8

Maaaaan. Summer is almost over. Which
means it's going to start raining all day soon,
which means it's back to zombie school and no
Frosty for a few months. They go vacation to the
mountains whenever the rainy season comes
around.

I am SO not looking forward to school. The only
thing more boring than eating brains for dinner
every night is learning all this useless stuff. Dad
put me in Ugh Therapy last year too which
means I get to sit around with a bunch of
villager zombies and sound out my ughs for 90
minutes twice a week.

Great. Just great.

Well I guess I should look at the dark side of things. Rain means I can go outside whenever I want. No more staring out the window while I wait for the sun to go down. And hey, I get to see Skelly-Lynn.

Day 9

Muahahaha! I totally tricked my dad into letting me go down to the lake earlier! I was all like:

"Hey dad, since it's raining can I go look for carrots?"

And he was like:

"Blah blah blah! Ugh I'm dad! About time you want to help out around here! Sure just be back for dinner!"

Dad sells carrots to the zombie pigmen down in the nether. They use them to get lots of regular pigs together so there's a better chance that lightning will strike one and make a new zombie pigman.

But ANYWAY while I was down there I found some sugar cane and tried some. It's like nothing I've ever tasted! Okay to be fair I've only ever had brains, flowers, fish and snow. But still.

Hey, I wonder how it would taste if I put some of this sugar cane in a snow slushie. Hmm…

Day 10

Dad took me to work with him today. He said
he wanted to show me what the real world was
like. Man, if I thought school was boring,
herding villagers is just... Uuuggghhhh.
Dad's the supervisor for this chunk's branch of
Zomb Eye Foods, so he spends a lot of time
looking for new villages and finding players to
trade with for villager spawn eggs. When we
were at work he took me out on the minecart
and we found a couple of villages. He said one
of them looked player-built but there were still
some villagers around.

Then he had to fire someone. God, even giving

someone horrible news sounds totally dull as a

zombie. It was literally just like...

"Step into my office."

steps in

"Listen, Grugghh. Uuuuuuggghhhhh, ugh....

Uugghh. You're fired."

"Ugh." *walks out moping*

Seriously nothing like in the movies. Woulda

been awesome if Grugghh punched a hole in the

ceiling to scare dad off with sunlight like in

"Ugh Brawn."

Day 11

Oh yeah! I'm skilled! GROUNDED YET
AGAIN! Is there some kind of world record for
this?

Dad caught me and Frosty eating sugary
slushies and he was M-A-D! I seriously thought
he was gonna just eat Frosty on the spot. And of
course he just made things worse when he tried
to tell my dad it wasn't that bad. Dad's face got
redder than redstone and Frosty was outta there.
I don't blame him.

Wait, let me stop for a second to just say – sugar
slushies are the bomb.

Back to dad: he seriously put me on a lead like some animal and dragged me back to the house. It's not like I wouldn't have went. He said I was grounded until school starts and that he was going to have a talk with Frosty's dad.

SIGH. What kind of lame zombie chick spends the last nights of her summer vacation stuck at home?

Day 12

Officially one week left of freedom. Or I guess confinement. Wow, that's ironic and sad.

I wonder why school starts on a Wednesday. Maybe it's the school's way of saying "hey kids, we know you're not used to getting up this early, so we'll make it a short week." Actually, you know, that probably is it.

Haven't had much to do all day. Just sitting around in my room... Helped mom organize the basement chests and took out the dirt. I saw Frosty while I was outside but dad was staring at me the whole time so I just gave him a friendly "ugh."

I don't know how I'm gonna make it another week before I can go outside again. And it's all because of that one sugar slushie. It was good but not grounded-for-a-week good. You know, I bet if mom and dad just tried some of this stuff they'd be alright with it.

Day 13

La la la. Another boring day of imprisonment.

I'm gonna make a list of things I want to try:

Mushroom stew – saw Steve eating this once, he freaked out and dropped the bowl when he saw me though.

Golden Apple – Hagatha said as long as I don't touch any potions of weakness it's okay.

Fried eggs – gotta be better than fried brains!

Cake – all that sugar….. mmmmm.

Whatever's inside of Frosty's head because it's certainly not BRAINS!!!

Frosty tried to sneak some snow into my window today. It was really nice, but he had to break it and put a new one in really quick since they don't open. Dad of course heard. I told him I had nothing to do with it... It was nice of him but just really, really not smart.

Wait, what IS in Frosty's head? Is that actually a pumpkin? Or is there more snow golem underneath?

Day 14

It's more snow golem.

Okay, so last night, Frosty shows up with

Zombrina and a couple of axes, and they literally

cut a hole in my wall to get me out of here! We

put the blocks back and ran for it. Dad was at

work but I didn't want mom to catch us either.

Especially not mom, since then she'd have to rat

me out and that's not fair for her.

I randomly asked Frosty about the pumpkin and

he just pulled it right off. His face is weird.

Kinda cute, like a little smiley face, but still

weird.

Anyway, we all hung out for a while, Frosty

made us some slushies, and then I went home.

Didn't want to risk dad catching me, and it

looked like it was gonna rain. Speaking of

which Frosty said they're leaving in a few days,

but he asked his parents and they said it was

alright if I came up to visit now and then.

Woohoo!

Day 15

Snuck out again to go see the Old Witch with
Zombrina. She just got back from her trip.
Hagatha made us some mushroom stew (one I
can cross of the list) and told us some stories. It
was really fun, and the stew was great. The
craziest one was one about my mom. I guess
back before I was born they were friends at a
monster high school and she came over to try
one of her potions, but she took the wrong one.
She drank a healing potion on accident and got
sick for a month! Poor mom!

Speaking of which, I was feeling kinda funny today so I told Zombrina I thought it was best for me to lay low for a while. I definitely don't want to get sick right before school starts. I guess I'll take the opportunity of being grounded to get some extra rest.

Day 16

Woah. Out of nowhere dad had a serious talk

with me today.

He finally told me why he's so strict about only

eating brains. He's worried that if I keep doing

weird non-zombie stuff it'll lead to more stuff,

like crafting and farming. He just doesn't want

me to get into bad zombie habits now.

It was really great to hear that. I like knowing
that dad's actually worried about me and not
just being a jerk. But him and mom just don't
get it. It's not a bad thing! And really neither is
farming – what's wrong with an infinite supply
of food? I'll admit crafting is pretty scary, that's
why we leave it to the professionals.

I feel kinda bad for mom and dad. They're so
stuck in the past that they can't enjoy anything
new. Times are changing. It's not all about
brains anymore... They even teach us that in
school.

Day 17

Last day of being grounded!

I'm actually kind of excited for school now. I was thinking about it yesterday when I was writing in here, and school's pretty great compared to what most zombies usually do. I'd much rather be learning about stuff than moping around ugh-ing all day.

Here's my class list this semester:

Zombie History II

Zombie Ethics and Financial Management

Gym

Zombie Hall

Public Ughing

Grave Economics

I'm most excited for Grave Ec. This year we're finally learning to make leather armor and some other fun stuff, at least that's what mom told me. She went to a ZTA meeting over the summer to talk to some of the teachers and stuff.

I heard we're also getting a new gym teacher. I hope they're nothing like the last one. All he did was make us do zombie exercises and chase each other around to "better prepare us for the real world."

Day 18

So, here it is. Frosty's up in the mountains and school has begun. Tis the season for rain all day long!

Skelly-Lynn sat with me on the bus in the morning and told me about her summer. She asked if I was okay because I was looking a little green, and I told her she looked like she lost some weight. Ha-ha, zombie and skeleton jokes.

We make the same jokes every year basically, not really to laugh but more like break the ice since we go all summer without seeing each other. I wish our schools weren't separate, I don't get why zombies can't learn with skeletons. Oh well, at least we get bus rides together. And sometimes gym if it's nice out. We have gym the same period so that's awesome.

Lunch was brain soup. Bleeechhh. I think I'm gonna go ask Hagatha for something a little tastier.

Day 19

Okay, something super crazy is going on at school!

Lunch today had two options... Brain patties or cooked steak.

Cooked steak. Not brains! Did the whole world suddenly turn upside down over the summer? First Zombrina, now even my school? Maybe times really *are* changing. I wanted to tell mom and dad but when I got home I realized dad might get really mad and make them only give me brains or something. So I'm just gonna keep quiet about it.

I'm proud to be part of a school like this. If no one ever changed anything we'd all still be mindlessly ughing around like freshly turned villagers. Who knows, maybe in a few years we'll learn to coexist with villagers and stop eating brains altogether!

Nah, I know that'd never happen. But still. I can't wait to see what the rest of this school year has in store for me.

Day 20

First Friday of the school year and we already had a sunny day! It just didn't want to rain so school was closed. Since it's the weekend I'm going go up to Frosty's tonight to say hi.

Oh yeah, speaking of the weather... That old villager zombie that was living with us is missing... He was annoying but I really hope he didn't get stuck outside. Maybe I'll look around for EXP tonight just to be sure.

Man, I sure miss being a little kid and not having to worry about the sun. I'd love to be able to just freely walk around outside whenever I want without worrying about bursting into flames. Why hasn't anyone invented something to just put over your head while you're outside? Well, my daylight sensor just turned off so I guess it's time to head out! Stay tuned for Frosty's House Adventures! Slushies and snowball fights surely await.

Day 21

Dear Diary... My head is spinning. And not
literally this time – boy that was a nightmare!
Okay, back on topic – yesterday when I was at
Frosty's... He told me he liked me. Don't get
me wrong, that little smiley face under the
pumpkin is super cute, but he's – well – I've
known him since he was made; it's just a little
weird. It almost feels like we're siblings. I
choked up when he told me and just said "yeah
right."

What do I do? What do I say? I don't want to hurt his feelings. I have to go back tonight and say something. I wish I saved up my allowance and bought a shovel so I could just dig my way up there, but doing it by hand would take all day.

Argh, I hate waiting. I wish Steve left his "/set time night" command block laying around more often.

Day 22

Okay. Not grounded, but still in trouble. Do I get bonus points for that?

So… After hanging out with Frosty again I realized I was just nervous last time… But my dad overheard us talking and dragged me home. He gave me a long lecture on why Snow Golems and zombies just can't be together. Basically, he kept mentioning that snow golems melt in the rain and walk in the sun, while it's the opposite for us. And then when I said "what about night time?" he just said "no! I forbid it! No more seeing Frosty!"

And that was that.

So, great. I just lost my best friend. It's not even about liking him. I'm just mad that my dad keeps super over-reacting to things. Sometimes I feel like I'm the only zombie who has a brain and doesn't eat them.

Meh. Just let it be tomorrow so I can go back to school already.

Day 23

Mmmm…. Apples!

Hagatha gave me a few apples when I went over after school. She even gave me a golden one. I made sure to stay faaaaaaar away from her splash potion chest. Super tasty!

In other news, I failed my first quiz at school. It was kinda rigged, so I'm not too bummed out about it. The questions were like, "When is the only time to not eat brains? A. Never B. When you're in the sun C. Never D. Never" …. I chose B and got it wrong. Well, I guess the extent of change in the school was that one day where we got different food.

Oh, I got to meet my new gym teacher. It's a she, and she's a Zombie Pigman... Er... Pigwoman? Whatever, she's cool – and really nice, unless you mess with her. One of my classmates wouldn't stop talking and she started yelling. All the Zombie Pigmen in the entire school came running to yell at the poor guy. Serves him right I guess!

Day 24

UGH. See? I'm practicing for my class.

UUUGGHHH.

I can't believe my dad! It was sunny out today
so Frosty came all the way down here just to say
hi to me and ask why I haven't been talking to
him. And dad just told him to go home!! AND
THEN IT STARTED RAINING!!!!

We all ran outside to see if he was okay but
luckily he had a few blocks of dirt with him, just
enough to cover his head. Dad went and got his
parents, they dug a hole down to our house and
dad made a little shed to keep them safe so he
could get home.

Seriously, what in the world was he thinking?

Frosty could have gotten hurt, or worse! UGH

UGH UGH!!!!!!

And of course when I freaked out my dad just

told me to go to my room. Whatever. At least

now we have a tunnel…

Day 25

Had gym today again. It was raining so I got to play with Skelly-Lynn. It was archery day, which she's awesome at, but I'm not so great at it so I mostly just watched. We talked about my dad and Frosty... And she said I should really talk to him.

She doesn't get it. Skeletons are much more careful than zombies about everything. They keep their distance from danger, don't go around turning villagers into skeletons, and know what it's like to be hunted down by something (wolves!). Skeletons can talk to their parents. I don't have that. Dad is just a ticking bomb…

Oh, there's dad now. He just got back from Frosty's house apologizing to his parents. I can only imagine what he said to them. What do you even say in that situation? Like "oh hey, sorry for almost hospitalizing your kid, no hard feelings right? Ugh brains!"

Day 26

Best day ever! I know I said that already but this is the new best day ever! Wait, did I say that? I don't know, whatever!

Dad came into my room last night with mom and they sat down to talk to me about stuff... I guess mom and Frosty's dad talked some sense into my dad, because he said he realized snow golems aren't all that bad. He said he was just trying to make my life easier.

They of course had to mention all the food I've been eating and getting grounded for, but I am too happy to get upset about that. I'm just so glad I can see Frosty again.

You know, this is the first time dad's ever changed his mind about something. Maybe while he's in a good mood I can get him to rethink the whole food thing? Not sure if I want to risk it or just enjoy good times while they're here…

Day 27

Woohoooooo! Weekend is here! It's supposed
to be sunny all weekend so Frosty and his dad
are spending some time down in The Village
and delivering some snow to Steve. Frosty's
gonna come over when the sun goes down. I
can't wait!

Even though I'm excited I feel a little weird. I
mean, not about Frosty – I just feel weird. Like
you feel after you eat a Player wearing smelly
leather armor. I went to see Hagatha about it
but she just gave me an apple and some baked
potatoes. She said I just had a stomach ache and
that would fix it.

Stomach ache? Pretty neat, zombies don't

usually get those. I guess that's what happens

when you eat a lot of non-brains food. It kind of

hurts but it's interesting at least hah!

Anndd there goes my daylight sensor. Time to

go wait for ol' Frosty. Bye Diary!

Day 28

Hagatha is in jail and I'm in the zombie hospital.
Today was crazy, that's the best way I can sum it
up. I'm still really nervous... Skeleton Jockeys
arrested Hagatha for feeding Player food to
zombie kids. I saw them taking her away and
one of them asked me if I ate anything from her.
I was scared so I said yes, and the next thing I
knew I was in an ambulance.

I guess some zombie scientists figured out why
we're not supposed to eat Player food. They
said it very slowly turns you into a Player, and
once you eat too much of it, it's hard to reverse
the process.

I'm scared. I'm really scared. I wish Frosty were here. Mom is crying and dad won't stop pacing back and forth.

I wish I listened to my dad. He was right all along. And so was mom… He was just looking out for me…

Day 29

Okay Diary, I'm ugh changed girl!

They had Steve come in to take ugh look at me.

Mom and dad had to pay him ugh diamond to

even step foot in the hospital. He doesn't like

zombies for obvious reasons, but money talks

ugh guess. He said I had ugh special

enchantment from eating that golden apple that

was changing me. All he had to do was enter

ugh command into his console and I was cured!

Ugh promise I'll never steal potatoes from him

ughgain. Thank Notch for Steve.

Since then I've eaten ugh lot of brains to try and get back to health. It's ugh really weird feeling. It's ugh little harder to think and sometimes ugh say "ugh" without even thinking ughbout it. Ugh.

Ugh don't really like it, but I'd rather ugh a little more than turn into ugh Player. Can't wait to tell Frosty the news!

Day 30

Ugh ugh uggghhh, ugh school. Went to see Frosty. Ugh told him ughbout ugh, he was really happy! He offered me ugh sugar slushie but ugh told him ugh was sticking to ugh diet of just brains for ugh while. Ugh packed ugh little snack so he didn't have to feel bad for not having any food for me.

Something exciting happened – ugh person from the Zombie College for Gifted Leathercrafters (ZCGL) came into my Grave Ec class. He saw my pink leather armor and was really impressed! Later ugh went down to the principal's office and my parents were there.

Ugh guess he wants me to enroll at the college next year as part of the early program instead of continuing with school.

Ugh don't want to leave Zombrina behind, but UGH how awesome is this! Ugh guess my life is going places.

Dad is proud of me.

Brains don't seem that bad.

The Adventure of Stevephen?

A (Rather Weird) Adventure Minecraft Story (Unofficial)

"Ten years ago, in a village near the outskirts of the Southern Kingdom, an Ender Dragon appeared. It wreaked havoc destroying the town and killing most of its inhabitants. Steve, the legendary hero of the Overworld, killed that dragon and saved the villagers. For many years they all lived in peace and safety until another dragon showed up threatening to destroy Overwold. Will Stephen, Steve's grandson, kill the dragon and save their world as his grandfather did?"

…Excerpt…

Chapter 1

The cicadas cried as the sun showered the Overworld with its warmth. In the middle of a forest, a man wearing a green beret endured the heat of the summer. He hid behind the bushes on the side of a wide dirt road. He seemed to be waiting for someone.

A few minutes passed by, a man carrying a rusted sword appeared from the other end of the road. The man with the green beret grinned and picked a stone off the ground. The man with the rusted sword come closer and the man wearing the green beret threw the stone at him.

Plock!

The stone hit the man straight on his forehead. He did not flinch or even notice that the stone shattered on his face. The man walked as if nothing happened.

"Hey, hey. This guy is weird. Let me throw another one."

Plock!

Another stone hit the man on the head. Just like before, it did not even faze him and he continued walking.

"Is his head made of steel? I'll put my everything in this shot. This one will definitely take his head off!" The man wearing the beret cocked his right hand as far as he can backwards and launched the stone his hand held towards the man who was walking on the dirt road.

PLACK!

The stone shattered into dust, but the man just continued walking.

"This is pissing me off!" The man in the bushes stood up from his position and jump in front of the man on the dirt road.

The man had a blank expression on his face. The presence of the man who appeared in front of him was not enough to make his eyes blink for a second.

The man sighed. "Okay, stone faced dude. You see, I've been trying to get your attention for a while now. And it seems that throwing stones on your head won't work."

"..."

"Are you mute? Are you deaf?" The stone throwing guy scratched his head.

"..."

He sighed once more and said, "I see. You're the silent stoic type, eh? I don't want to waste time, so could you just please walk in that direction?" The man pointed to the direction where he was sitting a while ago.

The silent man looked towards the direction where the man was pointing. He did not budge. He tilted his head a bit. After a second, he walked past the pissed man.

"I don't know if you knew there was a trap in there or what, but let's just get this over with quick." The man laid out his right hand. "Could you please hand over your belongings?"

"Why should I?"

His jaw dropped. "Woah! You can speak!" He laughed "It's just sad that you're a bit dumb, but that will make things easier. For your information, I'm what you call a 'thief'." The man brushed his hair upwards. "And as a thief, I will ask for your items, and you hand them to me with a smile. After that we're done. Got it? Easy right?!"

"Oh. I see." The silent man pulled his sword out.

"Woah, woah! Take it easy man!" The thief took a step back.

"Why?" The man said with a deadpan voice.

"I am a thief not a barbaric bandit. Thieves are gentlemen. We only seek your belongings and we love peace the most."

"But you lure people to traps?"

"Make no mistake, kind sir." The thief walked towards his trap and removed the plank that concealed it. "As you can see, I devised this trap to prevent people from harm. Look at the bottom of the trap."

The silent man walked towards the location of the thief and bent down. "I can't really see anything. The pit's too—" The thief shoved the man towards the pit.

"Haha! You're too nai—" The silent man got a hold of the thief's arm. Both fell in the pitfall. They spent a few seconds falling. And they landed on stacks of wool blocks.

"What do you know? You truly are a gentleman. There's a lot of wool here. It cushioned our fall." The man tapped the wool blocks that broke their fall.

"You dumbass! You should be the only one falling in this pit!" The thief stood.

"I can't really allow myself to have all the fun." The silent man laughed.

"Hey, hey! Stop laughing. You're creeping me out."

"I see. So, how does this work then? You get your victims to this pit, right? How will you get their belongings?"

"…" The thief looked up.

"Are you mute?" The silent man laughed again.

"Shut up!"

"So, how will you get their belongings?"

"I don't know! I haven't thought about it!"

"That's weird? And stupid?"

"Alright alright. I'm still training as a thief, okay? I never knew that this would be difficult! And just my luck. The first person that I met was an idiot like you!"

"Why blame me? People who call other people idiots are the idiots. That's what my grandfather told me always. Also, today's the first time that I've heard that thieves train."

"We do, dumbass. I bet your grandfather was as stupid as you."

"Dude, that's foul. You don't know my grandfather. Anyway, let's talk about that later. How do we escape here?"

"Well…"

"You also haven't thought about that, too?"

"I didn't! So what?! Just digging a pit this deep is tiring. What do you expect?"

"How did you climb back up?"

"I dug a tunnel of course!"

"And where is that tunnel now?"

"I filled it with dirt! Have you ever saw a pitfall trap with a way to escape?!"

"You have a valid point. But have you ever seen a pitfall with wool in it?!"

"You're really annoying."

Minecraft 101 Ultimate Secrets Handbook

Minecraft Book of Seeds: 35 Awesome Seeds